Comic Books: From Superheroes to
Manga

Joshua Hatch
AR B.L.: 3.7
Points: 0.5   MG

COMIC BOOKS

From Superheroes to Manga

by Joshua Hatch

Reading Consultant:
Timothy Rasinski, Ph.D.
Professor of Reading Education
Kent State University

Content Consultant:
Lawrence Klein, Esq.
Chairman
Museum of Comic and Cartoon Art

Red Brick™ Learning

Published by Red Brick™ Learning
7825 Telegraph Road, Bloomington, Minnesota 55438
http://www.redbricklearning.com

Library of Congress Cataloging-in-Publication Data
Hatch, Joshua, 1973–
    Comic books: from superheroes to manga / by Joshua Hatch; reading
consultant, Timothy Rasinski.
        p. cm.—(High five reading)
    Includes bibliographical references and index.
    ISBN 0-7368-5748-6 (soft cover)—ISBN 0-7368-5738-9 (hard cover)
    1. Comic books, strips, etc.—History and criticism. 2. Comic strip
characters. 3. Comic books, strips, etc.—Technique. I. Rasinski, Timothy
V. II. Title. III. Series.
PN6710.H37 2006
741.5'09—dc22
                                        2005011135

Created by Kent Publishing Services, Inc.
Designed by Signature Design Group, Inc.
Edited by Jerry Ruff, Managing Editor, Red Brick™ Learning
Red Brick™ Learning Editorial Director: Mary Lindeen

Printed in the United States of America.

1 2 3 4 5 6 11 10 09 08 07 06 05

Table of Contents

Superman has been a superhero since 1934.

CHAPTER 1

Super Idea

When do you have your best ideas?

While you shower? While you dream?

Some great ideas seem to come from nowhere.

What ideas have just "popped" into your head?

In His Dreams

It is 1934. Jerry Siegel, age 19, is asleep.
As he sleeps, he dreams. The dream is cool.
It's about a superhero. Then Jerry wakes up.
He writes down the dream as fast as he can.

Next, Jerry runs to his friend Joe's house.
Joe Shuster lives 12 blocks away. Jerry brings
sandwiches. He also brings his dream ideas.
Joe spends the rest of the day drawing.

By nightfall, Superman has been born.

Just Like Them

The ideas for Superman came from a dream.
But they also came from Jerry and Joe's lives.

For example, Superman has an **alias**
named Clark Kent. Clark is shy and wears
glasses. Jerry and Joe were shy and wore
glasses, too. Superman is **handsome**.
He is so strong that people call him the
"Man of Steel." Jerry and Joe also wanted
to be handsome and strong.

What about Superman's superpowers?
How did the young men think of those?
These two friends loved **science fiction**.
They loved science fiction books and movies.
Their ideas for Superman's powers came
from those books and movies.

---

alias (AY-lee-us): a made-up name used to hide who a
person is
handsome (HAN-suhm): very good looking
science fiction (SYE-uhnss FIK-shuhn): stories about
life in the future or on other planets

Joe Shuster shows the cover of a Superman comic book.

Not Much Luck

Jerry and Joe dreamed up many **comic strips**. They tried to sell them to newspapers and magazines. But they didn't have much luck. At first, no one even wanted Superman. But Jerry and Joe kept trying.

---

comic strip (KOM-ik STRIP): a group of cartoons that tell a story

Sold!

In 1938, Jerry and Joe finally sold Superman.
DC Comics printed Superman along with
other stories in *Action Comics*. Jerry and Joe
were paid $130. Readers loved Superman.
By the fourth **issue**, *Action Comics* was a hit.

A year later, DC Comics made a comic
book just about Superman. It was the
first comic book about only one **character**.
The comic sold
more than 1
million copies.

*A Superman comic
book from the 1930s*

---

issue (ISH-oo): a newspaper or magazine that is printed at
a certain time
character (KA-rik-tur): one of the people in a story

8

Superman Is Everywhere

Soon, Superman was everywhere. In 1940, *Adventures of Superman* came to radio. The next year, the first Superman cartoon movie was made. Other Superman movies and TV shows followed.

Jerry and Joe kept writing and drawing Superman comics. They even paid others to help. But Joe always drew Superman's face.

Superman was the first big comic book hit. In fact, Superman began the "Golden Age" of comic books. What might that mean?

This man is holding early issues of Batman, Superman, and Captain America comics.

— CHAPTER **2** —

Comic Ages

*What makes a comic book **popular**?*

Do adults read comic books?

Were there comic books before Superman?

How did comic books get started in the first place?

First Comics

People have told stories with pictures for thousands of years. Think of cave drawings. Cave drawings use pictures to tell a story. That's what comics do, too.

U.S. newspapers first began to print comics in the late 1800s. These comics were short. Many were funny. Some were about **politics**. Others told action stories.

---

popular (POP-yuh-lur): liked by many people
politics (POL-uh-tiks): a person's belief in how government should be run

The First Comic Books

The first comic books also were printed in the late 1800s. The comics in these books came from newspapers. Some comic books were in color. Others were black and white. Some comic books were given away for free. Others were sold.

In the 1930s, comic books came out with new stories and characters. Most stories were about **detectives** or science fiction. Few people read comic books at this time. Then DC Comics **published** Superman.

---

detective (di-TEK-tiv): a person who looks into crimes
publish (PUHB-lish): to produce written work so that people can buy it

Action Comics, *No. 1, with Superman,*
the "Man of Steel," started a new era in comic books.

The Golden Age

The Superman comic book started an **era**. *Action Comics,* No. 1, was the first really popular comic book.

Suddenly, **newsstands** were filled with comic books. Many were about superheroes. Some told stories about cowboys. Others told **horror** stories. Some made people laugh, like *Archie* comics. Everyone knew Archie and Jughead, the goofy teenage stars of this comic book.

---

era (IHR-uh): a period of time in history
newsstand (NOOZ-stand): a place that sells newspapers and magazines
horror (HOR-ur): intended to make you afraid

Spider-Man comics became very popular
after Superman was published.

End of an Era

In the 1940s, America was fighting in World War II (1939–1945). Many comic books told stories about the war. Sometimes superheroes fought the German **Nazis**.

But after World War II, readers lost interest in superheroes. People also didn't want to read about war anymore. Many comic books stopped printing. The Golden Age of comics ended.

Some comic books did stay popular. Comic books about **romance**, crime, and horror still sold well. But parents did not like these comics. Parents thought they taught children bad things.

Nazi (NOT-see): a group that ruled Germany from 1933–1945; Nazis killed millions of Jews, Gypsies, and other Europeans.
romance (ROH-manss): love between people

Comics Code

Comic book publishers did not want to anger parents. They also feared the government might **ban** their books. So in the 1950s, publishers created the Comics Code.

The Comics Code set rules for comic book stories and pictures. For example, comic books couldn't tell crime stories or show crimes. Comic books got a special stamp if they obeyed the code. Many stores would not sell comics without this stamp.

The Comics Code stamp appeared on the cover of comic books that followed the Comics Code.

---

ban (BAN): to forbid something

New Fears

During World War II, the United States invented the **atom bomb**. The United States dropped two atom bombs on Japan to help end the war. The terrible power of this bomb scared people, including kids.

In the late 1950s, comic books told stories about atom bombs. These stories were popular. They helped people deal with their fear of the bomb. Superheroes were created to protect people from these fears.

The Incredible Hulk was created from the kind of power used in atom bombs.

atom bomb (AT-uhm BOM): a powerful bomb that explodes with great force, heat, and light; it is made from splitting atoms

Modern Comics

During the 1960s, the United States was fighting in the Vietnam War (1954–1975). Another big concern was **civil rights**. People had questions about these and other matters.

Comic book artists wanted to tell stories about these matters. At first, the Comics Code still banned many topics. Then the Code was changed.

Soon comic book stories and characters began to change, too. Characters weren't totally good or evil. They didn't all have superpowers. The 1960s began the Silver Age of comics.

---

civil rights (SIV-il RITES): freedom for all people to enjoy life

A New Kind of Comic

In 1978, Will Eisner began a new kind of comic book. Eisner wrote comic books that were stories about everyday people. The stories were hundreds of pages long. Today we call this type of comic book a *graphic novel.*

Meet the Artists

Many people have created comic books. Some were not very good at it. But a few were great. They told stories and drew characters that are popular even today.

Which writers and artists are the best? Which ones made the greatest changes? How did they make such a difference?

Will Eisner works on a graphic novel.

*Stan Lee created many famous
comic book characters.*

— CHAPTER **3** —

Behind the Masks

Do you sing or play a sport? Do you draw?
Do you write? Everyone is good at something.
Everyone can get better at what they do, too.
Now you will meet some comic book artists who
became great!

Hero Maker

Stan Lee loved to write stories. Lee got his first job at Marvel Comics when he was almost 17. After working for only one year, he became the **editor** of Marvel Comics. Lee edited and wrote comic books for more than 30 years. He helped create many characters, too. They include Spider-Man, X-Men, and The Incredible Hulk.

---

editor (ED-uh-tur): a person who checks the content of a book before it is published

23

Everyday Hero

Spider-Man first appeared in comic books in 1962. He wasn't like other characters.

Spider-Man was a teenager. His real name was Peter Parker. Peter often felt lonely, angry, and **confused**. He wanted people to like him. Teenagers understood Peter. In many ways, he was like them.

The comic book hero Spider-Man was really a teenager named Peter Parker.

confused (kuhn-FYOOZD): not sure about something

Man of Darkness

Steve Ditko helped create Spider-Man.
Ditko draws dark, **eerie** art. He also drew
horror comics.

Ditko quit drawing Spider-Man after
four years. He doesn't say why he stopped.
Ditko is shy. He doesn't even like to have
his photo taken. Why do you think he
stopped drawing Spider-Man?

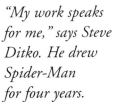

"My work speaks for me," says Steve Ditko. He drew Spider-Man for four years.

---

eerie (IHR-ee): scary or creepy

Kirby Comics

Stan Lee also worked with Jack Kirby.
Kirby drew many of the new superheroes.
The Fantastic Four was their first hero comic.
The four superheroes were Mr. Fantastic,
Invisible Girl, the Human Torch, and Thing.

Kirby and Lee also created The Incredible
Hulk. Like Peter Parker, the Hulk had
thoughts and feelings like everyday people.

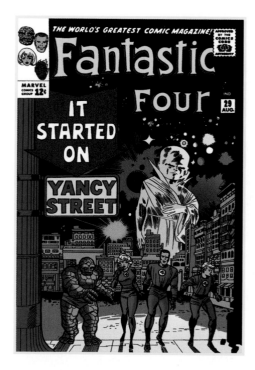

Jack Kirby and Stan Lee created The Fantastic Four *comics.*

Supermoney?

Not all comic book writers made it big when their comics did. Joe Shuster and Jerry Siegel sold Superman to DC Comics for only $130. When Superman became a radio, TV, and movie hit, DC Comics earned millions. Shuster and Siegel got nothing. They quit DC Comics and **sued**. They lost.

Shuster and Siegel never worked at DC Comics again. But, in the 1970s, DC Comics gave them more money for creating Superman. Now, Shuster and Siegel get **credit** for creating the Man of Steel.

What do you think it takes to draw a comic book? Do you want to try? The next chapter will show you how.

---

sue (SOO): to start a case against someone in a court of law
credit (KRED-it): praise; knowing that someone has done something

Trace this superhero on another sheet of paper.

CHAPTER 4

Drawing Comics

What will your superhero be like? Will it be a man?
A woman? A teenager? Will your hero have powers?
A cape? A mask? Get a pencil with a good eraser.
This time it's up to you.

Getting Started

One way to learn to draw is to **trace** over
other drawings. Get a piece of tracing paper.
Then trace over the superhero on the left.
Do not draw in this book! After you trace
the superhero a few times, try to draw the
character on your own.

---

trace (TRAYSS): to copy a picture by following lines you
see through a sheet of thin paper

What a Character!

Let's draw another comic book character. Call this character "Fabulous."

Start by drawing Fabulous as a stick figure like the one below. Make sure to show the shoulders, elbows, hips, and knees. Put Fabulous in an action **pose**.

pose (POHZ): a position of the body

Add the Main Body Parts

Now, add the main body parts. Draw the
main shapes for arms and legs over the stick
figure. Don't worry about the old lines.
You can erase them later.

Keep Going

Next, draw small **details** in the big shapes. Then use a pen to draw over the detail lines. When the ink is dry, erase the pencil marks. Now, add some color. Fabulous!

detail (DEE-tayl): a small part of a whole thing

Start a Comic!

It's time now to start your own comic strip. Let's use your superhero, Fabulous. Get a sheet of tracing paper. Draw three boxes in a row. These are your story **panels**.

Look at the stick figures to the right. In the first picture, Fabulous walks in a field. In the second picture, he falls over a cliff. In the third, he starts to fly.

Think of a story about Fabulous that uses these pictures. Trace one stick figure in each of your story panels to tell your story. Then add details to the pictures.

What happens to Fabulous next? Dream up some more ideas to continue the story. Draw them in more story panels. When you are done, you will have your own comic book.

---

panel (PAN-uhl): an area to draw a picture in

Comics Around the World

Not all comics began in the United States. Comic books are popular around the world. Read on to find out about manga!

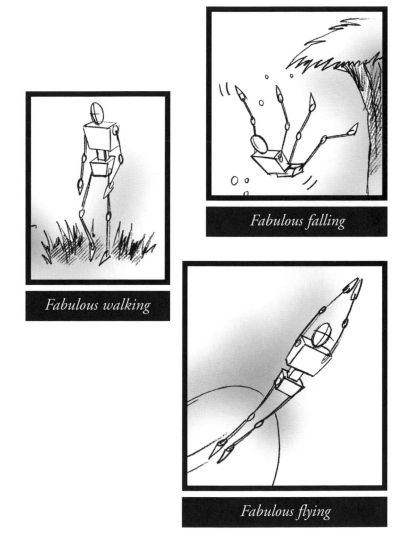

Fabulous falling

Fabulous walking

Fabulous flying

Akira Toriyama, a Japanese manga artist, did the art for the very successful DragonBall series.

CHAPTER 5

Manga Mania

Another comic book style is called manga.
Manga began in Japan in the 1940s.
You have probably seen manga characters.
They are in comics, movies, and video games.

Manga Style

Osamu Tezuka (oh-SAH-moo te-ZOO-kah) created the modern manga style. Manga characters have big eyes, spiky hair, and pointy noses and chins. People all over the world love manga comic books. One reason is that they come out weekly. You can read a new story every week.

---

manga (MANG-guh): a Japanese word for *comics*

Drawing Manga

Do you want to learn to draw manga?
It's not hard. Earlier we traced a superhero.
Let's do the same with a manga-style face.
Trace over the manga face below.

Manga Tips

How is the manga character different than
the superhero? The eyes are a big difference.
So is the shape of the head.

Manga and Eggs

The best way to draw manga is by practicing. The face is hardest. Here's an idea to help!

With an adult, hard-boil an egg. Once it cools, draw a face on it. Put the eyes in the middle of the egg. Add the mouth and nose. Use this head for practice.

Turn the egg in your hand. See how it looks facing you. See how it looks sideways. Try drawing these different **angles**.

angle (ANG-guhl): a way of looking at something

Practice, Practice, Practice!

The key to drawing comics is to practice.
Look around. Find something you want
to draw. Maybe it's a car, a friend, or a pet.

You can draw the object like a superhero.
You can draw it like manga. You're the artist!
Maybe you'll create the next Superman!

Epilogue

Comic Book Value

Some comic books are worth a lot of money. One comic book might be worth $10. Another copy of the same comic book might be worth $1,000! Each comic book's **condition** is important. An old, **rare** comic in great condition is worth a lot of money!

A comic book's value depends on its condition, its age, and how many copies there are.

In the past, *Action Comics,* No.1, cost 10¢. Today, a **mint** copy can sell for more than $86,000! Why? Because today there are only a few copies left. This makes *Action Comics,* No. 1, very valuable.

---

condition (kuhn-DISH-uhn): the look or state of a person, animal, or thing
rare (RAIR): not often seen or found
mint (MINT): as good as new

Comic Book Conditions

Comic book ratings tell their condition. Some ratings use numbers. Other ratings use **categories**. Here are some categories.

Mint: Perfect. There is nothing wrong with a comic book in mint condition.

Fine: Very little damage

Good: More signs of damage

Poor: Pages are missing from a comic book in poor condition.

Some collectors wear gloves when they read rare comics. Some won't open their comics at all. Collectors will pay more for comics that have never been opened or read!

---

category (KAT-uh-gor-ee): a group of things that have something in common

Glossary

alias (AY-lee-us): a made-up name used to hide who a person is

angle (ANG-guhl): a way of looking at something

atom bomb (AT-uhm BOM): a powerful bomb that explodes with great force, heat, and light; it is made from splitting atoms

ban (BAN): to forbid something

category (KAT-uh-gor-ee): a group of things that have something in common

character (KA-rik-tur): one of the people in a story

civil rights (SIV-il RITES): freedom for all people to enjoy life

comic strip (KOM-ik STRIP): a group of cartoons that tell a story

condition (kuhn-DISH-uhn): the look or state of a person, animal, or thing

confused (kuhn-FYOOZD): not sure about something

credit (KRED-it): praise; knowing that someone has done something

detail (DEE-tayl): a small part of a whole thing

detective (di-TEK-tiv): a person who looks into crimes

editor (ED-uh-tur): a person who checks the content of a book before it is published

eerie (IHR-ee): scary or creepy

era (IHR-uh): a period of time in history

handsome (HAN-suhm): very good looking

horror (HOR-ur): intended to make you afraid

issue (ISH-oo): a newspaper or magazine that is printed at a certain time

manga (MANG-guh): a Japanese word for *comics*

mint (MINT): as good as new

Nazi (NOT-see): a group that ruled Germany from 1933–1945; Nazis killed millions of Jews, Gypsies, and other Europeans.

newsstand (NOOZ-stand): a place that sells newspapers and magazines

panel (PAN-uhl): an area to draw a picture in

politics (POL-uh-tiks): a person's belief in how government should be run

popular (POP-yuh-lur): liked by many people

pose (POHZ): a position of the body

publish (PUHB-lish:) to produce written work so that people can buy it

rare (RAIR): not often seen or found

romance (ROH-manss): love between people

science fiction (SYE-uhnss FIK-shuhn): stories about life in the future or on other planets

sue (SOO): to start a case against someone in a court of law

trace (TRAYSS): to copy a picture by following lines you see through a sheet of thin paper

Bibliography

Beatty, Scott. *The Ultimate Guide to the Justice League of America*. New York: Dorling Kindersley, 2002.

Kobayashi, Junji. *Let's Draw Manga: Astro Boy*. Let's Draw Manga. New York: Digital Manga Publishing, 2003.

Owens, Thomas. *Collecting Comic Books: A Young Person's Guide*. Brookfield, Conn.: Millbrook Press, 1995.

Pellowski, Michael. *The Art of Making Comic Books*. Minneapolis: Lerner Publications, 1995.

Weiss, Harvey. *Cartoons and Cartooning*. Boston: Hougton Mifflin, 1990.

Useful Addresses

Museum of Comic and Cartoon Art
594 Broadway, Suite 401
New York, NY 10012

Internet Sites

Comic Book Conventions
http://www.comicbookconventions.com

Comicon.com
http://www.comicon.com

DC Comics
http://www.dccomics.com/dccomics/

Marvel Comics
http://www.marvel.com

Museum of Comic and Cartoon Art
http://www.moccany.org

TOKYOPOP
http://www.tokyopop.com

World Famous Comics Community
http://www.comicscommunity.com

Index